Table of Contents

★Copyright © 1989 ONDORISHA PUBLISHERS, LTD. All rights reserved.

★**Published by** ONDORISHA PUBLISHERS, LTD., 11-11 Nishigoken-cho, Shinjuku-ku, Tokyo 162

★**Sole Overseas Distributor:** Japan Publications Trading Co., Ltd.
P.O. Box 5030 Tokyo International, Tokyo, Japan.

★**Distributed in the United States by** Kodansha America Inc. through Farrar, Straus & Giroux,
19 Union Square West, New York, NY10003.
in British Isles & European Continent by Premier Book Marketing Ltd.,
1 Gower Street, London WC1E 6HA
in Australia by Bookwise International
54 Crittenden Road, Findon, South Australia 5023, Australia.

10 9 8 7 6 5 4 3 2

ISBN 0-87040-818-6

Printed and bound in Japan

Patchwork

5 Tips for Beginners

1 Study the pictures carefully — buy similar fabric.

2 Trace patterns. Paste patterns to cardboard with paper cement and cut out templates.

Place tracing paper on patterns given in book and trace. (You may xerox the patterns.)

tracing

paper

tracing paper   cardboard

Do not forget seam allowance.

3 Place template on wrong side of fabric and trace.

template

wrong side

sharp pencil

4 Cut fabric, adding 0.7 cm ($1/4''$) seam allowance. Referring to placement picture, sew together.

Take small stitches.

Use sharp scissors.

seam allowance

PATCH WORK

5 Finish project.

Fold seam allowance to wrong side and press with iron.

[To Applique]

background fabric

Place on background fabric and slipstitch in place.

[To Quilt]

backing
batting
pieced top

baste

Baste pieced top, batting and backing fabric.

Quilt.

ⓐ When finishing with backing fabric:

binding fabric

Bind seam allowance and slipstitch to backing.

[Two ways of binding project]

ⓑ When finishing with binding fabric:

Cut backing fabric adding binding width.

Bind and slipstitch.

Tea Cozy, Hot Plate Mat, Tea Mat

Instructions on P. 6

Rose Garden (actual size)

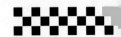
[Tea Cozy]

Materials······Scraps of patchwork fabric (5 kinds), Flower print fabric 90 cm × 1 m (35$\frac{1}{2}$″ × 39$\frac{3}{8}$″), Lining fabric 90 cm × 30 cm (35$\frac{1}{2}$″ × 11$\frac{3}{4}$″), Piping strip 2 m (78$\frac{3}{4}$″), Polyester stuffing

Finished size······Refer to illustration.

Directions

1) Cut fabric. Sew pieces in order a through e. Applique to front panel. Quilt.

2) With right sides together, sew front panel, back panel and gusset with piping strip and loop inserted. Turn inside ou

3) With right sides togehter, sew lining fabric.

4) Cut polyester stuffing in shape of 2) with 4 cm (1$\frac{5}{8}$″) thickness. Insert stuffing into 2).

5) Insert 3) into 4), fold hem and slipstitch lining fabric to hem

Patterns on P. 34

Number of pieces required:

a	pink	1
b	plaid	4
c	pink	4
d	flower	4
e	light pink	4

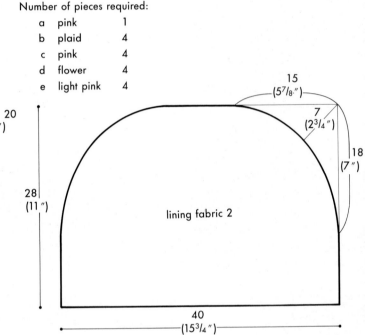

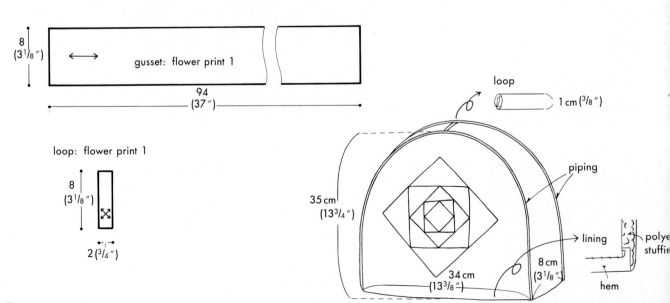

[Hot Plate Mat]

Materials······Scraps of patchwork fabric (5 kinds), flower print fabric 30 cm × 30 cm (11³⁄₄″ × 11³⁄₄″), Pre-quilted fabric 30 cm × 30 cm, Bias strip (1.2 cm ⁴⁄₈″) wide) 90 cm (35¹⁄₂″)

Finished size······approximately 27 cm (10⁵⁄₈″) in diameter

Directions

Follow same directions for Tea Mat.

Patterns on P. 34

0.7 cm (¹⁄₄″) seam allowance

Background fabric: Front panel······Flower print 1
Back panel······Pre-quilted fabric 1

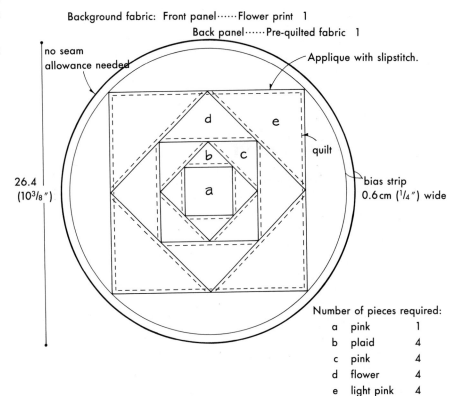

no seam allowance needed

Applique with slipstitch.

quilt

bias strip 0.6 cm (¹⁄₄″) wide

26.4 (10³⁄₈″)

Number of pieces required:
a	pink	1
b	plaid	4
c	pink	4
d	flower	4
e	light pink	4

[Tea Mat]

Materials (for 1)······3 kinds of patchwork fabric, flower print fabric 15 cm × 15 cm (5⁷⁄₈″ × 5⁷⁄₈″), Pre-quilted fabric 15 cm × 15 cm, Bias strip (1.2 cm ⁴⁄₈″) wide) 50 cm (19⁵⁄₈″)

Finished size······approximately 14 cm (5¹⁄₂″) in diameter

Directions

Cut fabric. Sew pieces in the order of a, b, c. Applique to front panel and quilt.
With wrong sides facing, sew bias strip around edge.

Patterns on P. 34

0.7 cm (¹⁄₄″) seam allowance

Background fabric: Front panel······Flower print 1
Back panel······Pre-quilted fabric 1

no seam allowance needed

Applique with slipstitch.

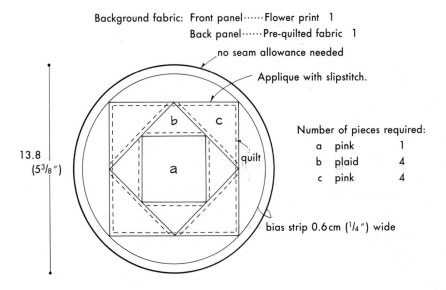

13.8 (5³⁄₈″)

quilt

Number of pieces required:
a	pink	1
b	plaid	4
c	pink	4

bias strip 0.6 cm (¹⁄₄″) wide

Pot Cover

Instructions on P. 10

Grandmother's Flower Garden (actual size)

Materials⋯⋯Patchwork fabric (refer to picture), Cotton fabric (left: polka dot, right: powder green) 90 cm × 80 cm ($35\frac{1}{2}''$ × $31\frac{1}{2}''$), Lining fabric 60 cm × 40 cm ($23\frac{5}{8}''$ × $15\frac{3}{4}''$), Batting 60 cm × 40 cm, Satin ribbon (0.9 cm ($\frac{3}{8}''$) wide) 120 cm ($47\frac{1}{4}''$)

Finished size⋯⋯17.5 cm ($6\frac{5}{8}''$) in diameter, 38 cm (15") tall

Directions

1) Cut fabric. Piece 7 hexagons to make one flower. Make 4 flowers. Applique 3 flowers, stems and leaves to background

( ) seam allowance

0.7 cm ($\frac{1}{4}''$) seam allowance for patchwork pieces

fabric. Applique remaining flower after side seams are sewn together.

2) Layer front panel, batting and lining. Quilt, leaving 5 cm (2") open on both sides.

3) Fold under seam allowance on front panel and lining as shown in illustration and slipstitch. Applique remaining flower motif on side seam. Quilt remaining edge.

4) Sew bias strip on top and bottom edge. Slipstitch ribbon carrier, insert ribbon and tie.

Patterns on P. 35

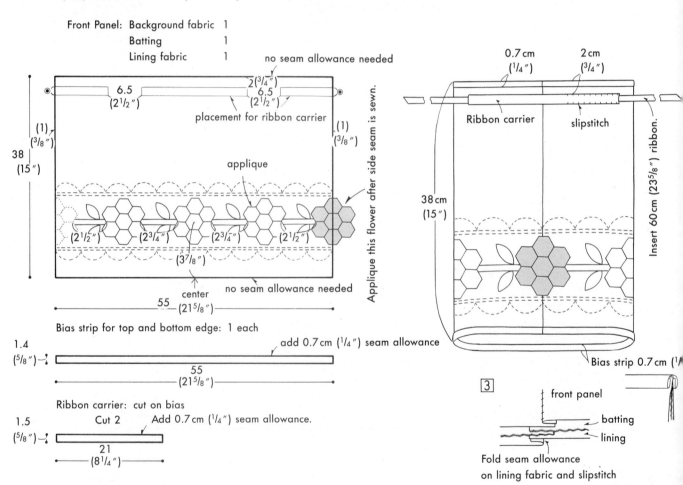

 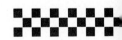
Materials⋯⋯Patchwork fabric (refer to picture), Solid color fabric (left: white, right: light blue) 90 cm × 1 m ($35\frac{1}{2}''$ × $39\frac{3}{8}''$), Lining fabric 90 cm × 1 m, Batting 110 cm × 60 cm ($43\frac{1}{4}''$ × $23\frac{5}{8}''$), 1 2 cm ($\frac{3}{4}''$) in diameter covered button

Finished size⋯⋯Refer to illustration.

Directions

1) Cut fabric. Sew pieces a through h. Make 4 and applique to top section. For side panel, sew pieces a through e, make 4 and applique.

2) Layer pieces in 1) with batting and quilt.

) With right sides together, sew side seams of side panel. With right sides together, sew side panel and top section. Sew lining fabric in the same manner. With wrong sides together, whipstitch seam allowance of outside section and lining.

Turn inside out. Sew bias strip on bottom edge.

4) Make loop and sew on top section. Cover button with 4.5 cm (1³/₄″) in diameter matching fabric and batting. Sew button on loop.

Seam allowance is 1 cm (³/₈″) unless indicated otherwise.

Patterns on P. 36

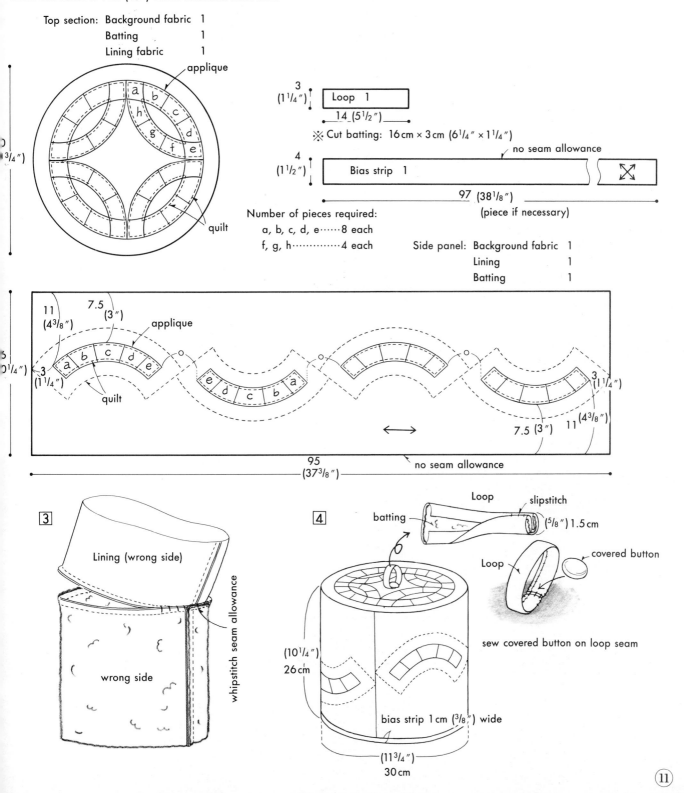

Top section: Background fabric 1
Batting 1
Lining fabric 1

applique

a b h c g d f e

quilt

3 (1¹/₄″)

Loop 1

14 (5¹/₂″)

※ Cut batting: 16 cm × 3 cm (6¹/₄″ × 1¹/₄″)

4 (1¹/₂″)

Bias strip 1

no seam allowance

97 (38¹/₈″)

(piece if necessary)

Number of pieces required:
a, b, c, d, e······8 each
f, g, h···········4 each

Side panel: Background fabric 1
Lining 1
Batting 1

11 (4³/₈″)   7.5 (3″)

applique

a b c d e

3 (1¹/₄″)

quilt

e d c b a

3 (1¹/₄″)

7.5 (3″)   11 (4³/₈″)

95 (37³/₈″)

no seam allowance

3

Lining (wrong side)

wrong side

whipstitch seam allowance

4

batting

Loop

slipstitch

(⁵/₈″) 1.5 cm

Loop

covered button

sew covered button on loop seam

(10¹/₄″) 26 cm

bias strip 1 cm (³/₈″) wide

(11³/₄″) 30 cm

11

Kitchen Cloths (Large & Small)

Instructions on P. 14

Triangle pattern variation (actual size)

[Kitchen Cloth (Large)]

Materials······Red cotton fabric (includes backing) 90 cm × 80 cm (35$\frac{1}{2}$″ × 31$\frac{1}{2}$″), Flower print fabric 90 cm × 30 cm (35$\frac{1}{2}$″ × 11$\frac{3}{4}$″), Red polka dot fabric 90 cm × 20 cm (35$\frac{1}{2}$″ × 11$\frac{3}{4}$″)

Finished size······56 cm × 56 cm (22″ × 22″) square

Directions

1) Cut fabric. Sew pieces together and make front panel.
2) Layer front panel and backing, quilt. Finish edges.

Patterns on P. 36

Number of pieces required:

a	flower print	54
	polka dot	27
b	red	9

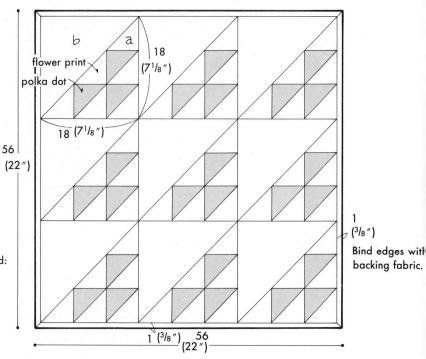

0.7 cm ($\frac{1}{4}$″) seam allowance

b a

flower print
polka dot

18 (7$\frac{1}{8}$″)

18 (7$\frac{1}{8}$″)

56 (22″)

1 ($\frac{3}{8}$″)

Bind edges with backing fabric.

1 ($\frac{3}{8}$″) 56 (22″)

Cut backing into 60 cm × 60 cm (23$\frac{5}{8}$″ × 23$\frac{5}{8}$″) square.

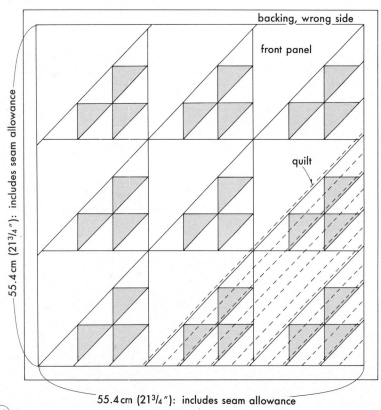

backing, wrong side

front panel

quilt

55.4 cm (21$\frac{3}{4}$″): includes seam allowance

55.4 cm (21$\frac{3}{4}$″): includes seam allowance

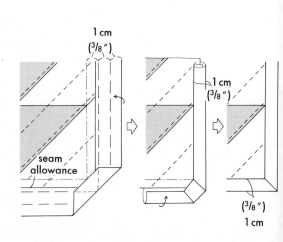

1 cm ($\frac{3}{8}$″)

1 cm ($\frac{3}{8}$″)

seam allowance

($\frac{3}{8}$″) 1 cm

[Kitchen Cloth (Small)]

Materials······Patchwork fabric, Red stripe fabric 50 cm × 50 cm
(19³/₄″ × 19³/₄″) square, Red polka dot (backing) 50 cm × 50 cm
square, #25 Red embroidery floss
Finished size······45 cm × 45 cm (17³/₄″ × 17³/₄″)

Directions

1) Cut fabric. Piece front panel. Sew pieced section to striped
   fabric and quilt.
2) Embroider.
3) Layer 2) with backing and finish edges.

Patterns on P. 36

0.7 cm (¹/₄″) seam allowance for patchwork pieces.

Number of pieces required:
 a light color 6
  dark color 3

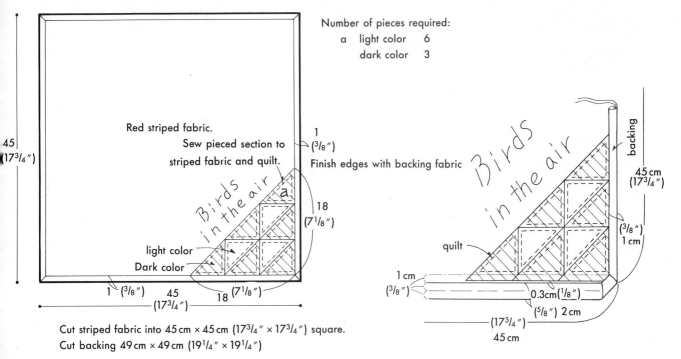

45
(17³/₄″)

Red striped fabric.
Sew pieced section to
striped fabric and quilt.

1
(³/₈″)
Finish edges with backing fabric

Birds in the air

a

18
(7¹/₈″)

light color

Dark color

1 (³/₈″) 45 18 (7¹/₈″)
(17³/₄″)

Cut striped fabric into 45 cm × 45 cm (17³/₄″ × 17³/₄″) square.
Cut backing 49 cm × 49 cm (19¹/₄″ × 19¹/₄″)

backing

Birds in the air

45 cm
(17³/₄″)

(³/₈″)
1 cm

quilt

1 cm
(³/₈″)

0.3cm(¹/₈″)
(⁵/₈″) 2 cm
(17³/₄″)
45 cm

Embroidery pattern (actual size)

Use three strands of embroidery floss.
(Refer to P. 47 for embroidering instructions)

outline stitch

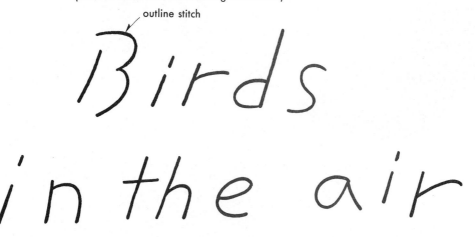

Birds
in the air

The gvift is small bvt love is all.

Rice Cooker Covers

Instructions on P. 10

Double Wedding Ring (actual size)

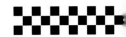

Materials······Blue cotton fabric 90 cm × 20 cm (35$\frac{1}{2}$″ × 7$\frac{7}{8}$″), Blue polka dot fabric 90 cm × 10 cm (35$\frac{1}{2}$″ × 4″), Border print 90 cm × 10 cm, White cotton 60 cm × 30 cm (23$\frac{5}{8}$″ × 11$\frac{3}{4}$″), Backing fabric 70 cm × 40 cm (27$\frac{1}{2}$″ × 15$\frac{3}{4}$″), Batting 70 cm × 40 cm, #25 Blue embroidery floss

Finished size······31 cm × 62 cm (12$\frac{1}{8}$″ × 24$\frac{3}{8}$″)

Directions

1) Cut fabric. Applique patchwork motif.
2) Layer 1) with batting and quilt.
3) With right sides together, sew backing fabric and border fabric.
4) With wrong sides together, layer 2) and 3). Fold border fabric to front side and slipstitch. Quilt border.

1 2

Patterns on P. 32

0.7 cm ($\frac{1}{4}$″) seam allowance

(12$\frac{1}{4}$″)
31
border fabric A: blue
($\frac{3}{4}$″)
2

white

applique

a

b

c

62
(24$\frac{3}{8}$″)

58
(22$\frac{7}{8}$″)

border fabric B: blue

Number of pieces req
a   polka dot
b   border print blue
c   blue

2
($\frac{3}{4}$″)

27
(10$\frac{5}{8}$″)
2 ($\frac{3}{4}$″)   2 ($\frac{3}{4}$″)

* Cut backing fabric 33 cm × 64 cm (13″ × 25$\frac{1}{4}$″).
  Cut batting 31 cm × 62 cm (12$\frac{1}{4}$″ × 24$\frac{3}{8}$″).
* Cut two each of the following: border fabric A 32.5 cm × 3.5 cm (12$\frac{3}{4}$″ × 1$\frac{3}{8}$″), border fabric B 59.5 cm × 3.5 cm (23$\frac{3}{8}$″ × 1$\frac{3}{8}$″)

batting

applique

quilt, 2 strands of embroidery floss

1 cm ($\frac{3}{8}$″)

1 cm ($\frac{3}{8}$″)

1 cm

59.4 cm (23$\frac{3}{8}$″) (includes seam allowance)

($\frac{5}{8}$″)   ($\frac{3}{8}$″)   ($\frac{5}{8}$″)
1.7 cm   ($\frac{5}{8}$″) 1.7 cm   1.7 cm

28.4 cm (11$\frac{1}{8}$″) includes seam allowance

3 4

1 cm   2 cm
($\frac{3}{8}$″) ($\frac{3}{4}$″)

border fabric B (wrong side)

backing fabric (right side)

($\frac{1}{4}$″)0.7 cm

border fabric A (wrong side)

($\frac{1}{4}$″)
0.7 cm

2 cm ($\frac{3}{4}$″)

2 cm ($\frac{3}{4}$″)

quilt, 2 strands of embroidery flos

Materials······a. Black plaid, black flower print 90 cm × 5 cm (35½″ × 2″) each, b. Solid color fabric (top: white, bottom: black) 90 cm × 20 cm (35⅞″ × 7⅞″), Polka dot (upper: white, lower: beige) 90 cm × 1 m (35½″ × 39⅜″), Backing fabric ? cm × 1 m, Thin batting 110 cm × 70 cm (43¼″ × 27½″), Ribbon (top: 1.4 cm (⅝″) wide, 60 cm (23⅝″); bottom: ? cm (1″) wide, 30 cm (11¾″))

Finished size······60 cm × 45 cm (23⅝″ × 17¾″)

Directions

Cut fabric. Make front panel by sewing sections A, B, C with patchwork pieces.

Layer front panel with batting. Quilt along inner edge.

Layer back panel and batting. Baste. With right sides together, sew front and back panel leaving opening for hanger. Trim excess fabric around shoulder area. Turn inside out.

With right sides together, sew backing fabric. Trim excess fabric around shoulder area.

Insert 3) into 4) and bind lower edge. Finish hanger opening, attach ribbon.

Patterns on P. 37

All seam allowances except lower edge and bias strip are 0.7 cm (¼″).

Fabric used in top cover: polka dot on white, bottom cover: polka dot on beige.

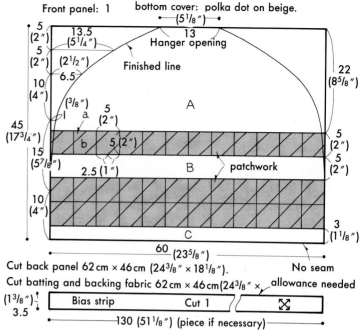

Cut back panel 62 cm × 46 cm (24⅜″ × 18⅛″).
Cut batting and backing fabric 62 cm × 46 cm (24⅜″ × allowance needed

Bias strip	Cut 1	

130 (51⅛″) (piece if necessary)

Number of pieces required:

a	plaid	36
	flower print	36
b	solid	
	(top: white	
	bottom: black)	36

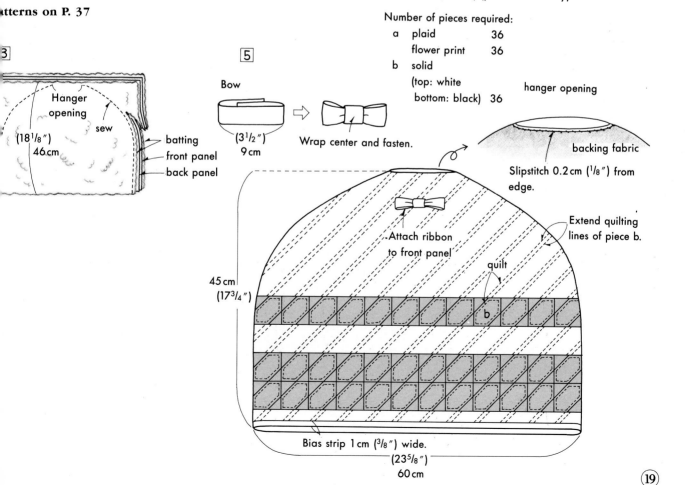

③

Hanger opening

(18⅛″) 46 cm

sew

batting
front panel
back panel

⑤

Bow

(3½″) 9 cm

Wrap center and fasten.

hanger opening

backing fabric

Slipstitch 0.2 cm (⅛″) from edge.

Attach ribbon to front panel

Extend quilting lines of piece b.

quilt

b

45 cm (17¾″)

Bias strip 1 cm (⅜″) wide.

(23⅝″) 60 cm

Oven Toaster Cover
& Potholder

Instructions on PP. 22, 23

Star variation (actual size)

Materials······Brown print fabric 90 cm × 5 cm (35$\frac{1}{2}$″ × 2″), Pre-embroidered fabric 90 cm × 20 cm (35$\frac{1}{2}$″ × 7$\frac{7}{8}$″), Off-white print fabric 30 cm × 10 cm (11$\frac{3}{4}$″ × 4″), Striped fabric (5 cm (2″) wide stripes) 90 cm × 90 cm (35$\frac{1}{2}$″ × 35$\frac{1}{2}$″), Backing fabric 90 cm × 60 cm (35$\frac{1}{2}$″ × 23$\frac{5}{8}$″), Batting 90 cm × 60 cm, #25 Brown embroidery floss
Finished size······Refer to illustration.

Directions

1) Cut fabric. Applique patchwork motifs to front and back panels.

2) Layer 1) with batting and quilt. Quilt top and back section in the same way.

3) With right sides together, sew front, sides and back sections. With right sides together, sew top to previously pieced section. Turn inside out and quilt along top edge (near seams). Sew backing fabric in the same way and insert into quilted piece. Bind bottom edge. Embroider front panel.

Seam allowance for patchwork is 0.7 cm ($\frac{1}{4}$″).

Patterns on P. 34

All other seam allowances are 1 cm ($\frac{3}{8}$″) unless otherwise indicated.

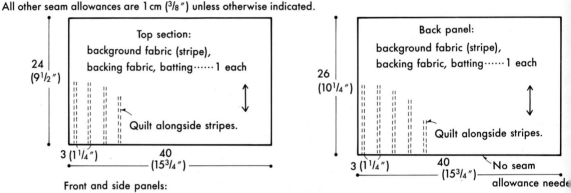

Number of pieces required:

a	brown	24
b	pre-embroidered fabric	12
c	pre-embroidered fabric	12
d	off-white	3

Embroidery Pattern (actual size)
Use 2 strands of embroidery floss in outline stitch.
(Refer to P. 47 for embroidery instructions.)

SawTooth

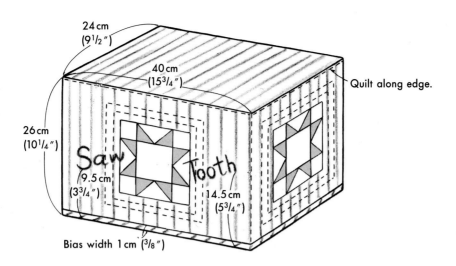

24 cm
(9¹/₂″)

40 cm
(15³/₄″)

Quilt along edge.

26 cm
(10¹/₄″)

Saw   Tooth

9.5 cm
(3³/₄″)

14.5 cm
(5³/₄″)

Bias width 1 cm (³/₈″)

Potholder······P. 20

Materials (for 1)······Small pieces of fabric for patchwork, bias strip, loop, Backing fabric 20 cm × 20 cm (7⁷/₈″ × 7⁷/₈″), Batting 40 cm × 20 cm (15³/₄″ × 7⁷/₈″)

Finished size······Refer to illustration.

Directions

1) Cut fabric. Sew pieces together to make front section.

2) Layer front section and batting. Quilt.

3) Layer 2), batting and backing fabric. Cut excess seam allowance and trim corners into curves. Bind edges with bias strip. Be sure to insert loop when slipstitching bias strip.

Patterns on P. 33

0.7 cm (¹/₄″) seam allowance

b
a
c
d
quilt

18
(7¹/₈″)

18
(7¹/₈″)

* 1 backing fabric 20 cm × 20 cm (7⁷/₈″ × 7⁷/₈″)
  2 batting   20 cm × 20 cm (7⁷/₈″ × 7⁷/₈″)

1.4
(¹/₂″)

piping strip 1,

70 cm (27¹/₂″), piece if necessary

1.4
(¹/₂″)

loop 1

10
(4″)

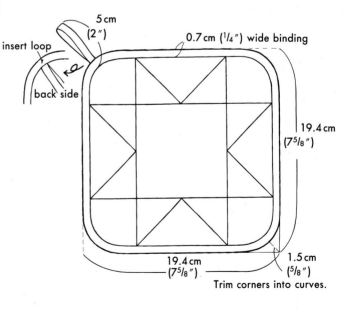

5 cm
(2″)

insert loop

back side

0.7 cm (¹/₄″) wide binding

19.4 cm
(7⁵/₈″)

19.4 cm
(7⁵/₈″)

1.5 cm
(⁵/₈″)

Trim corners into curves.

Mini Tapestry

Instructions on P. 26

Star variation (actual size)

Materials:

Top: a–d Scraps of brown cotton fabrics (refer to photo), e Cream color cotton fabric 90 cm × 20 cm ($35^1/_2$″ × $7^7/_8$″), Dark green backing fabric 60 cm × 60 cm ($23^5/_8$″ × $23^5/_8$″), Batting 60 cm × 60 cm, #25 Dark brown embroidery floss

Bottom: b–d, f Scraps of green cotton fabric, a Scraps of cream color cotton fabric (refer to photo), g Dark green cotton fabric 90 cm × 40 cm ($35^1/_2$″ × $15^3/_4$″), Cream color backing fabric 60 cm × 60 cm ($23^5/_8$″ × $23^5/_8$″), Batting 60 cm × 60 cm, #25 Beige embroidery floss

Finished size······56 cm × 56 cm (22″ × 22″)

Directions

1) Cut fabric. Sew pieces together to make front panel.
2) Embroider on pieces e (top) or g (bottom).
3) Layer front panel, batting and backing fabric. Quilt. Finish edges.

Patterns on P. 35

0.7 cm ($^1/_4$″) seam allowance

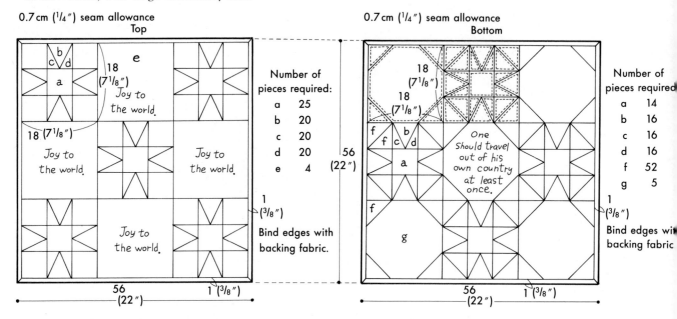

Top

Number of pieces required:

a	25
b	20
c	20
d	20
e	4
	1 ($^3/_8$″)

Bind edges with backing fabric.

Bottom

Number of pieces required

a	14
b	16
c	16
d	16
f	52
g	5
	1 ($^3/_8$″)

Bind edges with backing fabric

Cut backing fabric and batting 60 cm × 60 cm ($23^5/_8$″ × $23^5/_8$″)

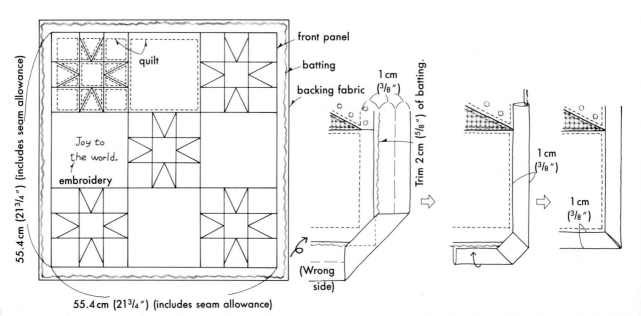

55.4 cm ($21^3/_4$″) (includes seam allowance)

55.4 cm ($21^3/_4$″) (includes seam allowance)

front panel

batting

backing fabric

1 cm ($^3/_8$″)

Trim 2 cm ($^5/_8$″) of batting.

1 cm ($^3/_8$″)

1 cm ($^3/_8$″)

(Wrong side)

Embroidery Pattern (actual size)
  Use backstitch unless otherwise indicated.
  (Refer to P. 47 for embroidery instructions.)
  Use 3 strands of embroidery floss.

Top

Joy to the world. French Knot

Bottom

One should travel out of his own country at least once. French Knot

Wallhanging

Instructions on P. 30

Tree (actual size)

 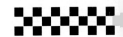

Materials······a–h Scraps of patchwork fabric (refer to photo),
Light brown cotton fabric 90 cm × 60 cm (35^1/$_2$″ × 23^5/$_8$″),
Backing fabric 60 cm × 60 cm(23^5/$_8$″ × 23^5/$_8$″), Batting
60 cm × 60 cm
Finished size······approximately 54 cm × 54 cm (21^1/$_4$″ ×
21^1/$_4$″)

Directions

1) Cut fabric. Sew pieces together.
2) Sew borders and make front panel.
3) Layer front panel, batting, backing fabric and quilt. Trim
   excess seam allowance.
4) Make loops and insert when binding edges.

Patterns on P. 38, 39

Seam allowance for patchwork pieces is 0.7 cm (^{1}/$_4$″).
Seam allowance for border pieces is 1 cm (^{3}/$_8$″).
Use light brown cotton fabric for all other pieces except
pieces a through h.

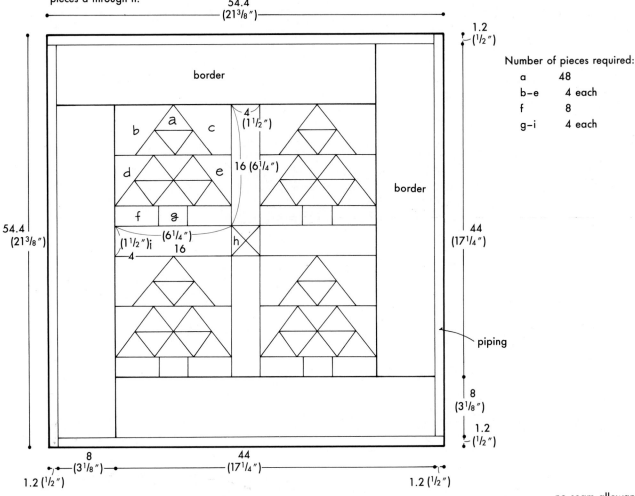

Number of pieces required:

a	48
b–e	4 each
f	8
g–i	4 each

Cut backing fabric and batting 58 cm × 58 cm (22^7/$_8$″ × 22^7/$_8$″).

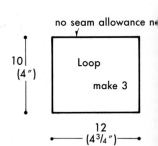

Loop
make 3

no seam allowance needed

Piping strip: make 4

4.8 (1^7/$_8$″)

55 (21^5/$_8$″)

10 (4″)

12 (4^3/$_4$″)

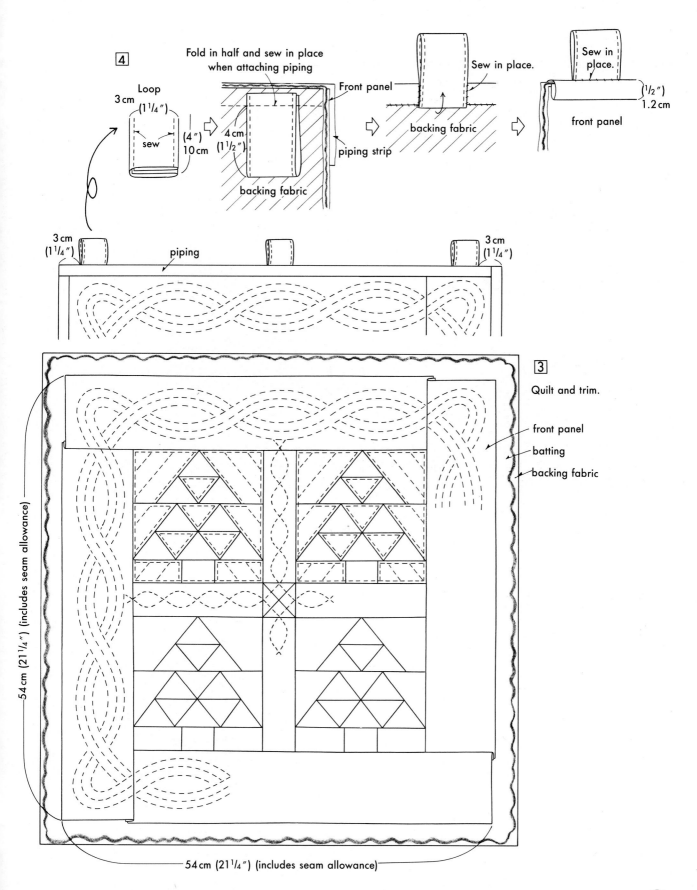

4

Loop

3 cm
(1¼")

sew

(4")
10 cm

Fold in half and sew in place
when attaching piping

Front panel

4 cm
(1½")

backing fabric

piping strip

Sew in place.

backing fabric

Sew in
place.

front panel

(½")
1.2 cm

3 cm
(1¼")

piping

3 cm
(1¼")

3

Quilt and trim.

front panel

batting

backing fabric

54 cm (21¼") (includes seam allowance)

54 cm (21¼") (includes seam allowance)

31

Telephone Cover

Instructions on P. 18

Maple Leaf (actual size)

Star variation······Potholder

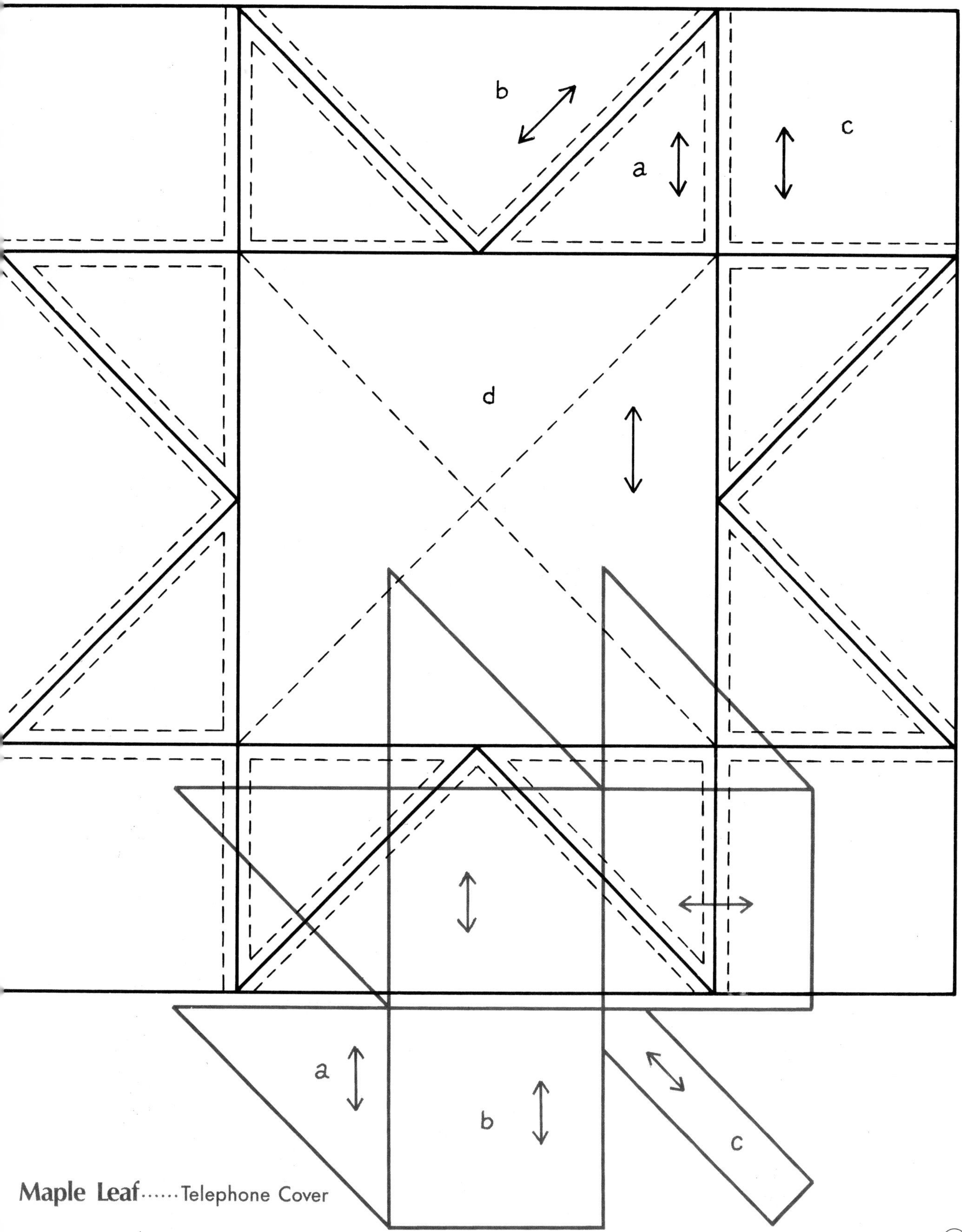

b

a

c

d

Maple Leaf······Telephone Cover

a

b

c

Rose Garden......
Tea Cozy, Hotplate Mat, Tea Mat

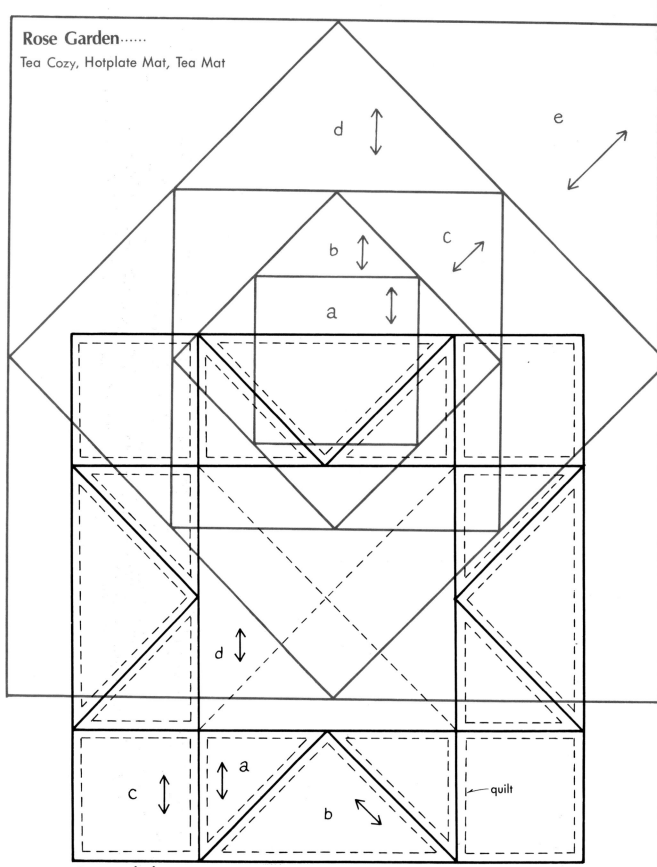

d

e

b

c

a

d

a

c

b

quilt

Star variation......Oven Toaster Cover

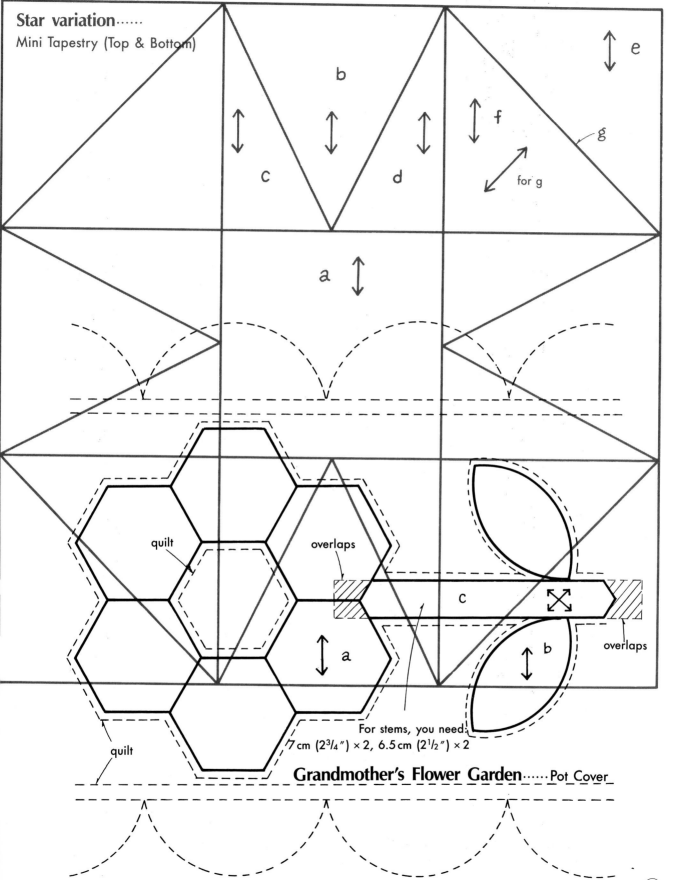

Star variation······
Mini Tapestry (Top & Bottom)

e

b

f

g

c

d

for g

a

quilt

overlaps

a

c

overlaps

quilt

b

For stems, you need:
7 cm ($2^3/_4$″) × 2, 6.5 cm ($2^1/_2$″) × 2

Grandmother's Flower Garden······Pot Cover

quilt

Triangle variation······Kitchen Cloths

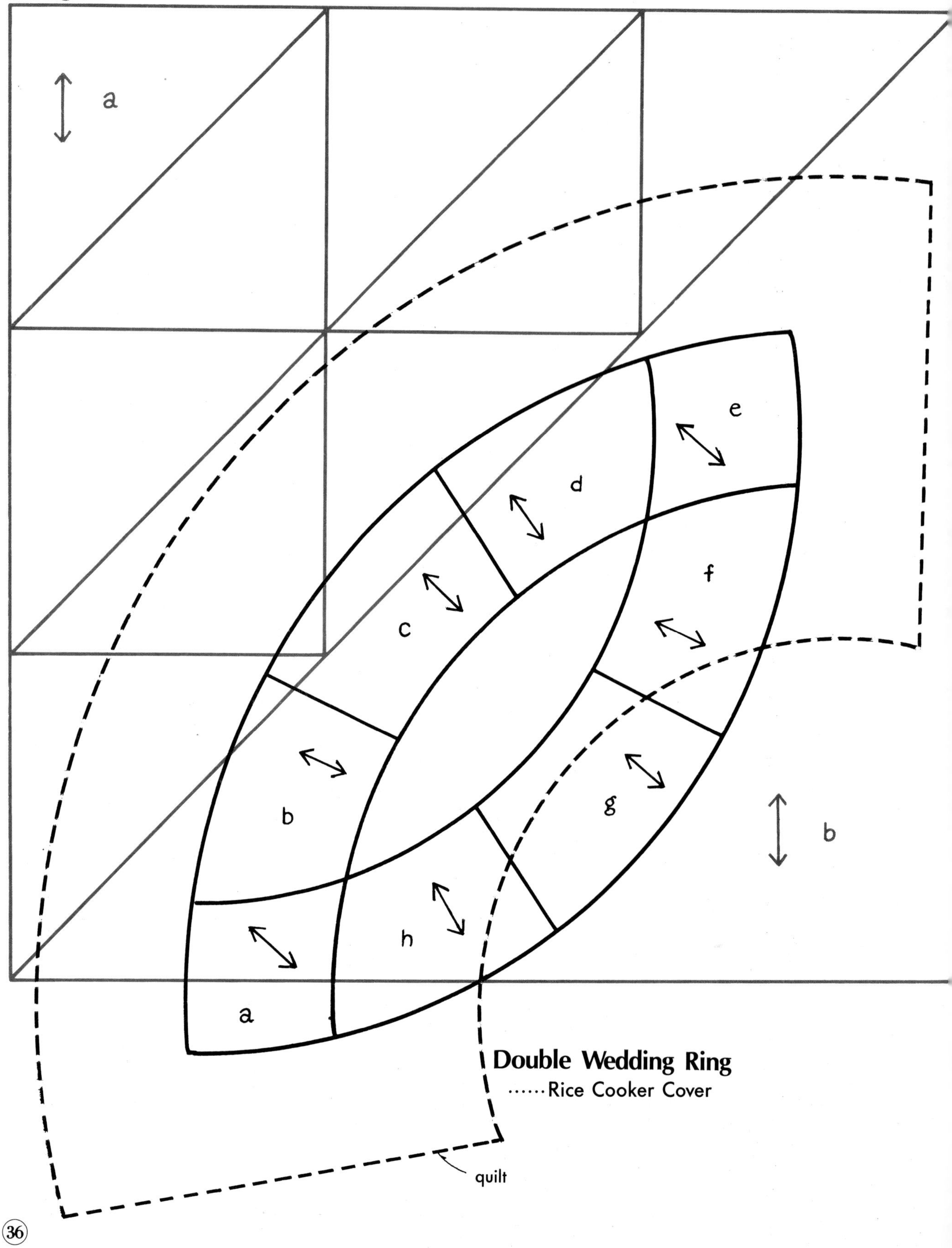

a

b

a

b

c

d

e

f

g

h

Double Wedding Ring
······Rice Cooker Cover

quilt

Log Cabin·····Small Tote Bag

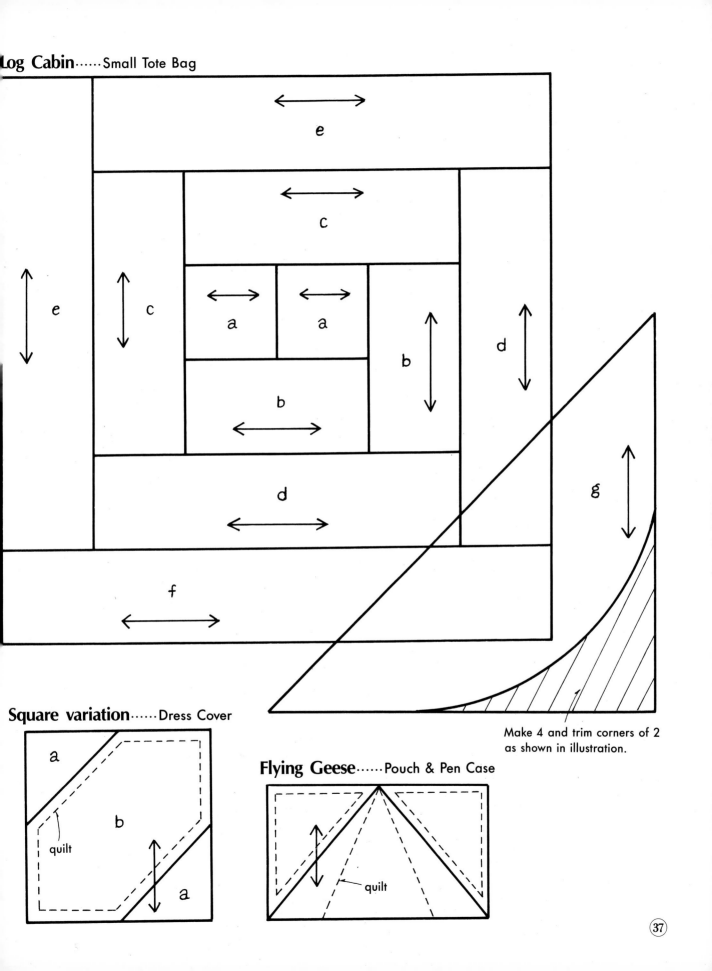

e

c

a   a

b

b

d

e

c

d

f

g

Make 4 and trim corners of 2
as shown in illustration.

Square variation·····Dress Cover

a

b

quilt

a

Flying Geese·····Pouch & Pen Case

quilt

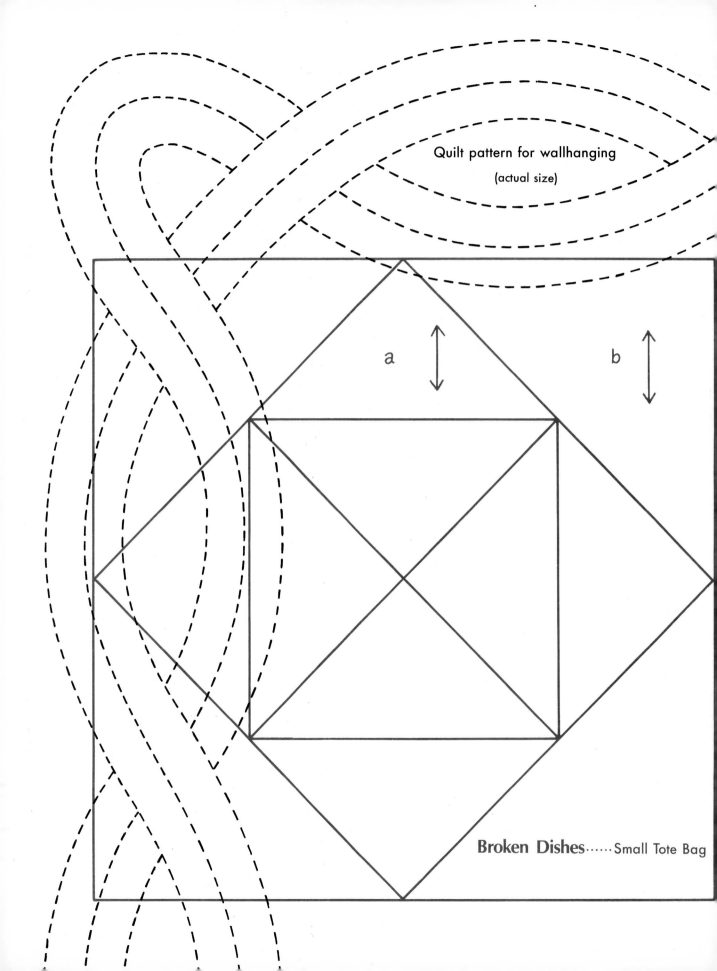

Quilt pattern for wallhanging
(actual size)

a

b

Broken Dishes......Small Tote Bag

Tree······Wallhanging

b

a

quilt

c

d

e

f

g

i

h

h

Ribbon······Tote Bags

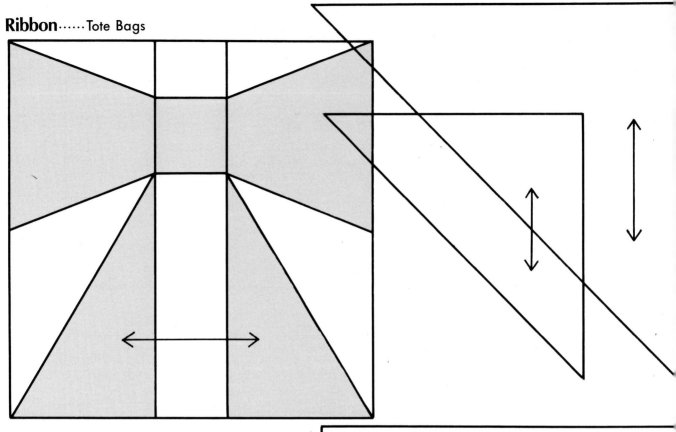

Kaleidoscope······Variety of Tissue Covers

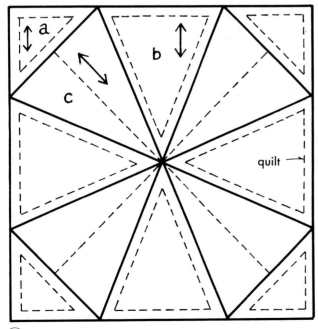

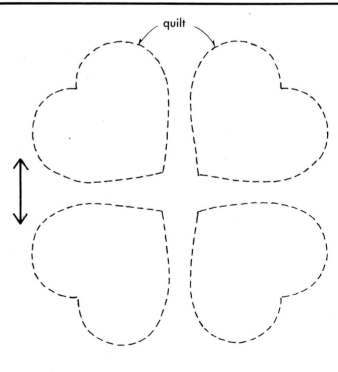

quilt

quilt

Dolls

Instructions on P. 42

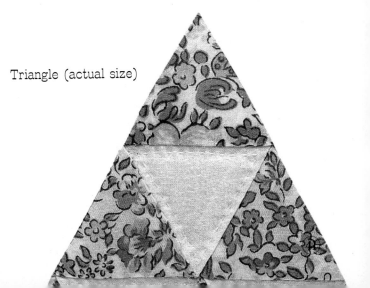

Triangle (actual size)

Materials·····a, c back panel fabric: (left: yellow, center: light rose, right: light pink) 30 cm × 30 cm (11³/₄″ × 11³/₄″), b Scraps of patchwork fabric (refer to photo), Scraps of dark brown and tan color for applique use Batting 30 cm × 20 cm (11³/₄″ × 7⁷/₈″), Polyester stuffing, #25 Navy blue and ivory embroidery floss

Finished size·····Refer to illustration.

Directions

1) Cut fabric. Applique a and c. Piece b. Center two sections and sew.

2) Layer 1) and batting. Quilt. Embroider designated areas. Trim excess batting and b fabric.

3) With right sides together, sew 2) and back panel fabric, leaving opening. Turn inside out and stuff with polyester stuffing. Sew opening. Add color to cheeks using blush powder.

Patterns on P. 43

Applique pattern (actual size)
(Refer to P. 47 for embroidery instructions.)
0.5 cm (¹/₄″) seam allowance

quilt

dark brown

tan

Use backstitch and fill in from outer line inwards navy blue, 2 strands

shoes

dark brown

blush powder

navy blue

ivory

Use 2 strands and backstitch:

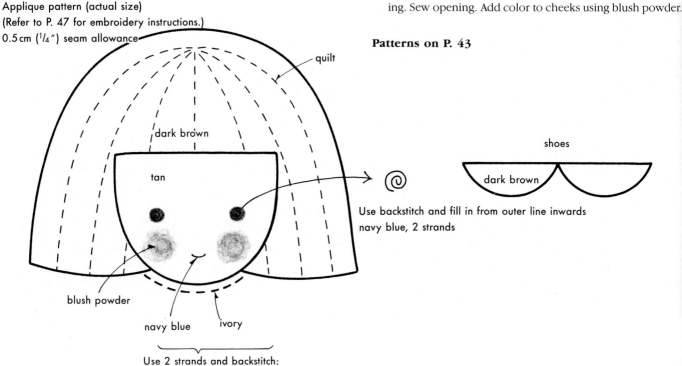

1   applique

a

patchwork

b

sew

sew

c

applique

2   batting

trim excess fabric and batting

seamline

quilt alongside seamline

3

(8¹/₂″) 21.5 cm

polyester stuffing

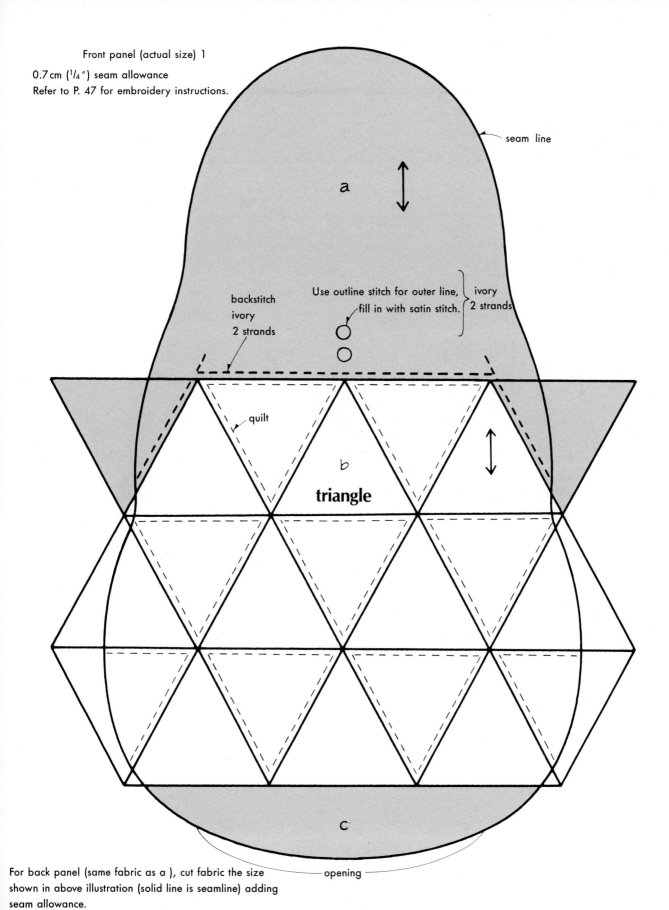

Front panel (actual size) 1

0.7 cm (¹/₄″) seam allowance

Refer to P. 47 for embroidery instructions.

seam line

a

backstitch
ivory
2 strands

Use outline stitch for outer line,
fill in with satin stitch.

ivory
2 strands

quilt

b

triangle

c

For back panel (same fabric as a), cut fabric the size
shown in above illustration (solid line is seamline) adding
seam allowance.

Cut batting 15 cm × 24 cm(5⁷/₈″ × 9¹/₂″).

opening

Cushion (pair)

Instructions on P. 46

Sunbonnet Sue (actual size)

Materials······Scraps for applique (refer to photo), Cotton print 90 cm × 40 cm ($35^1/_2$″ × $15^3/_4$″), Solid cotton fabric (top: beige, bottom: light brown) 90 cm × 40 cm, #25 Brown embroidery floss, 30 cm ($11^3/_4$″) zipper, Nude cushion 40 cm × 40 cm ($15^3/_4$″ × $15^3/_4$″)

Finished size······38 cm × 38 cm (15″ × 15″) (excluding ruffles)

Directions

1) Cut fabric. Applique Sunbonnet Sue motif to background fabric and embroider.

2) Gather ruffle. Sew appliqued piece to front panel, centering it carefully and insert ruffle.

3) Apply zipper to back panel.

4) Gather ruffle a. With right sides together, sew front and back panels inserting ruffle.

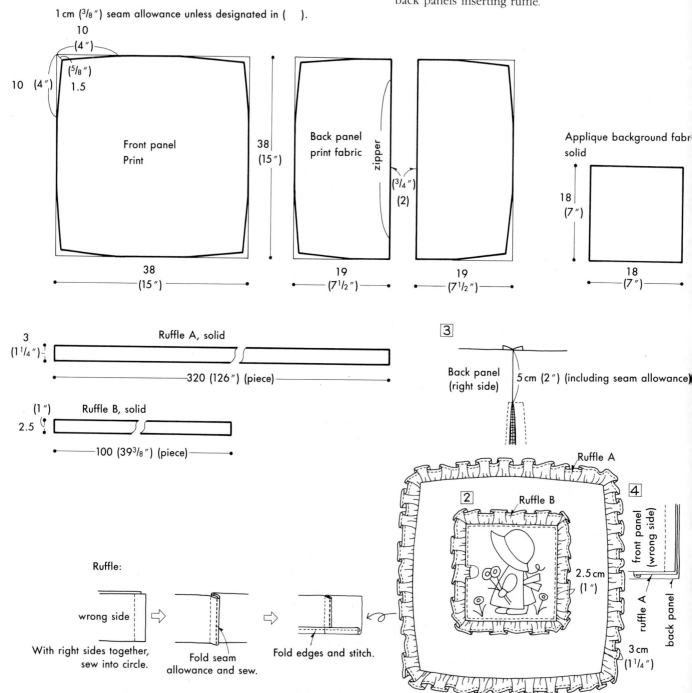

1 cm ($^3/_8$″) seam allowance unless designated in ( ).

10 (4″)
($^5/_8$″) 1.5
10 (4″)

Front panel Print
38 (15″)
38 (15″)

Back panel print fabric — zipper
($^3/_4$″) (2)
19 ($7^1/_2$″)
19 ($7^1/_2$″)

Applique background fabric solid
18 (7″)
18 (7″)

3 ($1^1/_4$″) — Ruffle A, solid — 320 (126″) (piece)

(1″) — Ruffle B, solid
2.5 — 100 ($39^3/_8$″) (piece)

3 Back panel (right side) 5 cm (2″) (including seam allowance)

Ruffle A
Ruffle B
2
4
2.5 cm (1″)
front panel (wrong side)
ruffle A
back panel
3 cm ($1^1/_4$″)

Ruffle:
wrong side
With right sides together, sew into circle.
Fold seam allowance and sew.
Fold edges and stitch.

Sunbonnet Sue

(applique pattern, actual size)
0.3 cm–0.7 cm ($\frac{1}{8}$" – $\frac{1}{4}$") seam allowance
Use 4 strands of embroidery floss.
For top cushion, use applique pattern symmetrically.

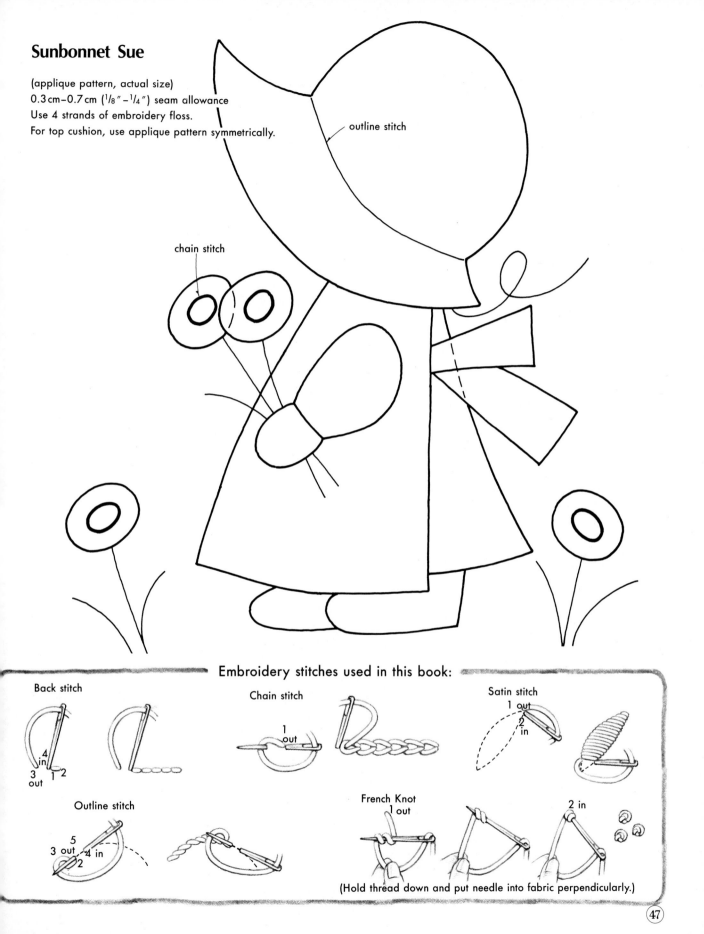

outline stitch

chain stitch

Embroidery stitches used in this book:

Back stitch

4
in
3   1   2
out

Chain stitch

1
out

Satin stitch

1 out
2
in

Outline stitch

5
3 out   4 in
2

French Knot

1 out

2 in

(Hold thread down and put needle into fabric perpendicularly.)

Drawstring Purses and Mini Tote Bags

Instructions for Drawstring Purses on P. 50
and Mini Tote Bags on P. 51

Log Cabin (actual size)

Broken Dishes (actual size)

 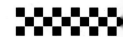
Materials······Plaid cotton fabric (left: gray, right: pink) 90 cm × 20 cm ($35\frac{1}{2}'' \times 7\frac{7}{8}''$), Polka dot cotton fabric and flower print fabric 30 cm × 10 cm ($11\frac{3}{4}'' \times 4''$), each, Solid cotton fabric (left: yellow, right: light brown) 60 cm × 10 cm ($23\frac{5}{8}'' \times 4''$), Lining fabric 40 cm × 20 cm ($15\frac{3}{4}'' \times 7\frac{7}{8}''$), Satin ribbon (1 cm ($\frac{3}{8}''$) wide) 50 cm ($19\frac{5}{8}''$), 1 Metallic bead

Finished size······17 cm × 21.5 cm ($6\frac{5}{8}'' \times 8\frac{1}{2}''$)

0.7cm ($\frac{1}{4}''$) seam allowance unless otherwise indicated in (   ).

Directions

1) Cut fabric. Sew pieces together and make front and bac panel.
2) With right sides together, sew sides and bottom of 1).
3) With right sides together, sew side seam of lining bag. Cente seam as shown in illustration 3) and sew bottom. Layer wit 2) and sew bottom seam allowance. Turn inside out.
4) With right sides together, sew drawstring section, leavin an opening for inserting ribbon.
5) With right sides together, sew 3) and 4). Turn inside ou and slipstitch to lining.
6) Stitch drawstring carrier line, insert ribbon and metalli bead. Tie end.

Patterns on P. 3

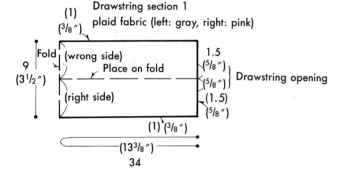

Drawstring section 1
(1) ($\frac{3}{8}''$)
plaid fabric (left: gray, right: pink)

Fold
(wrong side)
Place on fold
(right side)
9 ($3\frac{1}{2}''$)
1.5 ($\frac{5}{8}''$) ($\frac{5}{8}''$) Drawstring opening
(1.5) ($\frac{5}{8}''$)
(1) ($\frac{3}{8}''$)
($13\frac{3}{8}''$)
34

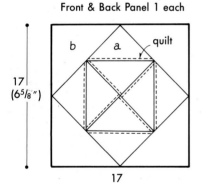

Front & Back Panel 1 each

b a quilt
17 ($6\frac{5}{8}''$)
17 ($6\frac{5}{8}''$)

Number of pieces required:
a polka dot 4
   flower print 4
   solid (left: yellow
          right: light brown) 8
b plaid (left: gray
          right: pink 8

Cut lining fabric 36 cm × 19 cm ($14\frac{1}{8}'' \times 7\frac{1}{2}''$).
Cut batting 20 cm × 20 cm ($7\frac{7}{8}'' \times 7\frac{7}{8}''$); you need 2.

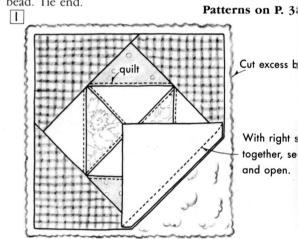

quilt
Cut excess b
With right s together, se and open.

Piece 8 a's. Center pieced section on batting and quilt. Attach b to quilted section and sew through batting. Trim batting to size of pieced section.

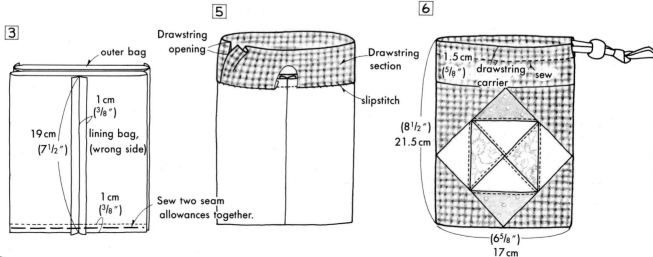

3
outer bag
1 cm ($\frac{3}{8}''$)
19 cm ($7\frac{1}{2}''$)
lining bag, (wrong side)
1 cm ($\frac{3}{8}''$)
Sew two seam allowances together.

5
Drawstring opening
Drawstring section
slipstitch

6
1.5 cm ($\frac{5}{8}''$) drawstring carrier sew
($8\frac{1}{2}''$) 21.5 cm
($6\frac{5}{8}''$) 17 cm

Materials……Scraps of patchwork fabric a–g (refer to photo), solid cotton fabric (left: pink, right: purple) 90 cm × 30 cm (35½″ × 11¾″), Lining fabric 50 cm × 30 cm (19⅝″ × 11¾″), Batting 90 cm × 30 cm

Finished size……21 cm × 22 cm (8¼″ × 8⅝″)

Directions

1) Cut fabric. Sew pieces a through g and quilt g. Trim excess batting.

2) Layer back panel with batting. With right sides together, sew front and back panel. Trim corners into curves and trim excess seam allowances.

3) With right sides together, sew side seam of lining bag. Center side seam. Cut corners into curves and sew using 0.7 cm seam allowance. Layer outer bag and lining bag. Sew bottom seam allowances together. Turn inside out.

4) Bind top edges with piping strip. Attach handles.

Patterns on P. 37

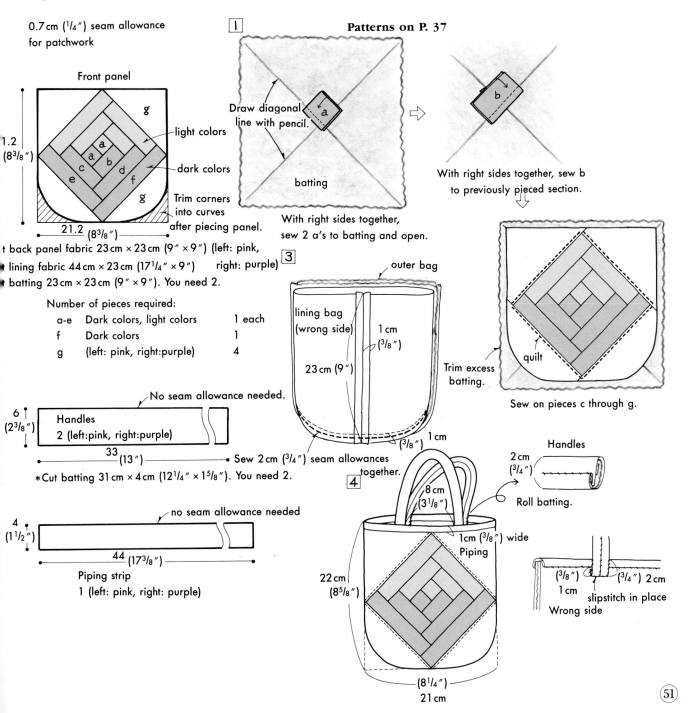

0.7 cm (¼″) seam allowance for patchwork

Front panel

light colors

dark colors

Trim corners into curves after piecing panel.

1.2 (8⅜″)

21.2 (8⅜″)

Draw diagonal line with pencil.

batting

With right sides together, sew 2 a's to batting and open.

With right sides together, sew b to previously pieced section.

Cut back panel fabric 23 cm × 23 cm (9″ × 9″) (left: pink, right: purple)

Cut lining fabric 44 cm × 23 cm (17¼″ × 9″)

Cut batting 23 cm × 23 cm (9″ × 9″). You need 2.

Number of pieces required:
- a–e Dark colors, light colors 1 each
- f Dark colors 1
- g (left: pink, right:purple) 4

outer bag

lining bag (wrong side)

1 cm (⅜″)

23 cm (9″)

Trim excess batting.

Sew on pieces c through g.

quilt

No seam allowance needed.

6 (2⅜″)

Handles
2 (left:pink, right:purple)

33 (13″)

Sew 2 cm (¾″) seam allowances together.

*Cut batting 31 cm × 4 cm (12¼″ × 1⅝″). You need 2.

no seam allowance needed

4 (1½″)

44 (17⅜″)

Piping strip
1 (left: pink, right: purple)

8 cm (3⅛″)

22 cm (8⅝″)

1cm (⅜″) wide
Piping

(8¼″)
21 cm

Handles

2 cm (¾″)

Roll batting.

(⅜″) (¾″) 2 cm
1 cm

slipstitch in place

Wrong side

Puffy Bags

Instructions on P. 54

Puff (actual size)

Materials······Scraps of fabric for puffs and drawstring ends, Fabric for opening section and drawstring 40 cm × 110 cm (15³/₄″ × 43¹/₄″), Lining and piping fabric 90 cm × 20 cm (35¹/₂″ × 7⁷/₈″), Batting 110 cm × 60 cm (43¹/₄″ × 23⁵/₈″), Polyester stuffing, Cotton cording (0.6 cm (¹/₄″) in diameter) 112 cm (44¹/₈″)

Finished size······24 cm × 26.5 cm (9¹/₂″ × 10¹/₂″)

Directions

1) Cut fabric.
2) Referring to illustrations, make puffs.
3) Sew opening section. Attach with 2) and sew into bag.
4) Make cording carrier. Sew handles to wrong side of bag. Insert cotton cording from both openings. Attach ends to cording.

Seam allowance is 1 cm (³/₈″) unless otherwise indicated.

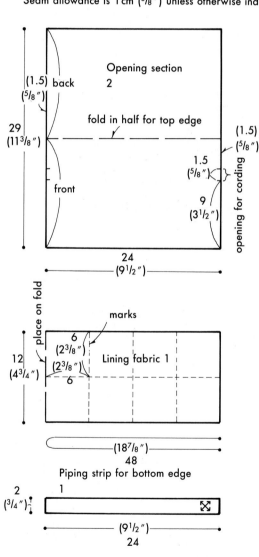

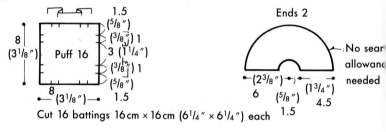

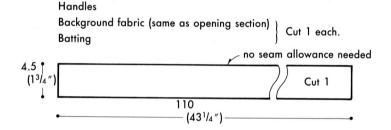

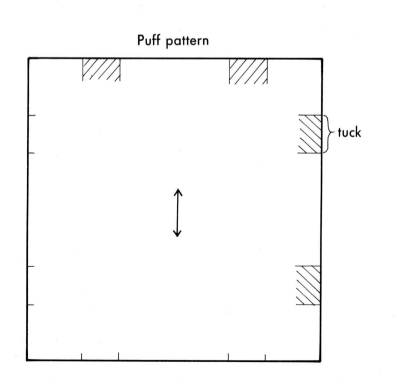

Puff pattern

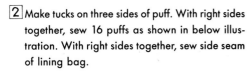

2 Make tucks on three sides of puff. With right sides together, sew 16 puffs as shown in below illustration. With right sides together, sew side seam of lining bag.

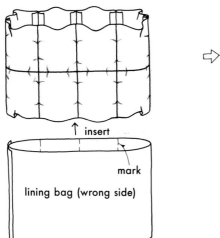

↑ insert

mark

lining bag (wrong side)

Align marks on lining bag and puff seams. Sew on puff seams.

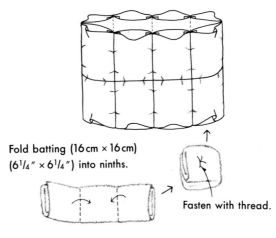

Fold batting (16 cm × 16 cm) (6¼″ × 6¼″) into ninths.

Fasten with thread.

Make tucks on top and bottom edge and baste. Turn outside in and sew bottom edge and bind with piping strip. Turn inside out.

lining

baste

1 cm (³⁄₈″) Cut corners.

piping (1 cm (³⁄₈″) wide)

3 With right sides together, sew both side seams of opening section, leaving an opening for drawstrings. With right sides together, sew with 2), fold back and slipstitch to lining bag.

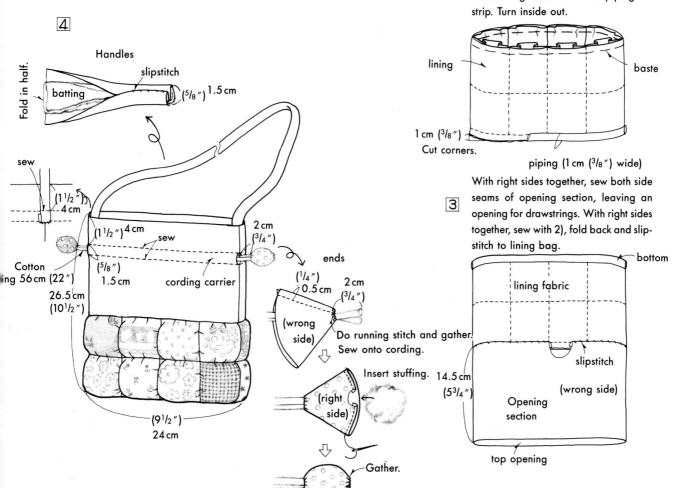

4

Handles

Fold in half.

batting

slipstitch

(⁵⁄₈″) 1.5 cm

sew

(1½″) 4 cm

(1½″) 4 cm

sew

2 cm (³⁄₄″)

Cotton ing 56 cm (22″)

(⁵⁄₈″) 1.5 cm

cording carrier

26.5 cm (10½″)

ends

(¼″) 0.5 cm

2 cm (³⁄₄″)

(wrong side)

Do running stitch and gather. Sew onto cording.

(9½″) 24 cm

Insert stuffing.

(right side)

Gather.

bottom

lining fabric

slipstitch

(wrong side)

14.5 cm (5³⁄₄″)

Opening section

top opening

Tote Bags

Instructions on P. 58

Ribbon (actual size)

Arabian Bean Salad

Serves 6-8

Materials······Scraps of print fabric (2 kinds) and off-white fabric, Beige polka dot 90 cm × 20 cm (35½″ × 7⅞″), Solid color cotton fabric (top: moss-green, bottom: gray-green) 90 cm × 50 cm (35½″ × 19⅝″), Backing fabric 90 cm × 40 cm (35½″ × 15¾″), Lining fabric 90 cm × 40 cm, Thin batting 90 cm × 50 cm

Finished size······Refer to illustration.

Directions

1) Cut fabric. Piece front panel.
2) Layer front panel, back panel, bottom section with batting

and backing fabric. Quilt.

3) With right sides together, sew front and back panels and bottom section. Fold bottom section in half as shown in illustration. Fold lining bag bottom section in the same way. Sew outer bag and lining bag side seams separately for 10 cm. Then layer outer and lining bags and sew together. Turn inside out.

4) Make handles. Attach to wrong side of outer bag. Fold seam allowance on top edge of lining bag and slipstitch to outer bag.

0.7 cm (¼″) seam allowance

Front Panel
Background fabric, backing fabric, batting······1 each

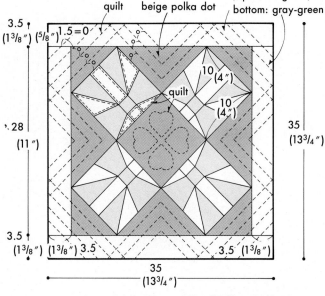

Cut lining fabric 76 cm × 37 cm (29⅞″ × 14½″)

Back Panel
Background fabric (top: moss-green, bottom: gray-green), backing fabric, batting······1 each

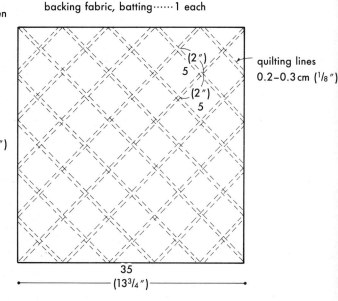

Bottom section
Background fabric (top: moss-green, bottom: gray-green), backing fabric, batting······1 each

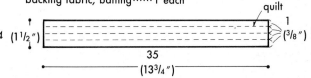

Handles
(top: moss-green, bottom: gray-green)······6

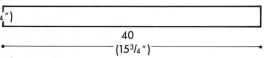

Cut batting 42 cm × 2 cm (16½″ × ¾″). You need 6.

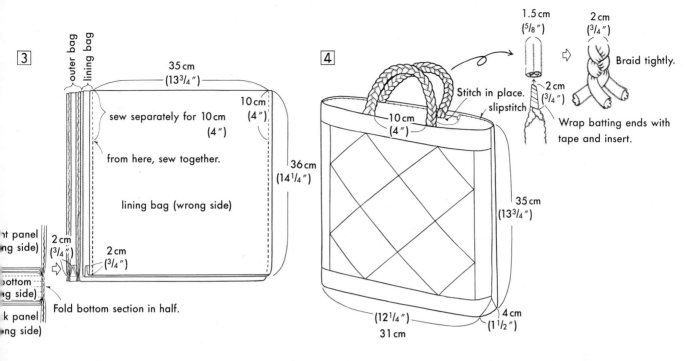

3

outer bag
lining bag

35 cm
(13¾")

10 cm
(4")

sew separately for 10 cm
(4")

from here, sew together.

lining bag (wrong side)

36 cm
(14¼")

nt panel
ng side)

2 cm
(¾")

2 cm
(¾")

ottom
g side)

Fold bottom section in half.

k panel
ng side)

4

1.5 cm
(⅝")

2 cm
(¾")

Braid tightly.

Stitch in place.
slipstitch

10 cm
(4")

2 cm
(¾")

Wrap batting ends with
tape and insert.

35 cm
(13¾")

(12¼")
31 cm

4 cm
(1½")

Pincushion······P. 64

aterials······Scraps of fabric for front and back sections,
olyester stuffing

nished size······Refer to pattern.

Directions

1) Cut fabric. Sew pieces together to make front section.
2) With right sides together, sew back section leaving opening.
3) With right sides together, sew front and back section. Turn inside out and stuff. Sew opening.

Star variation

pattern
0.7 cm (¼") seam allowance

front section

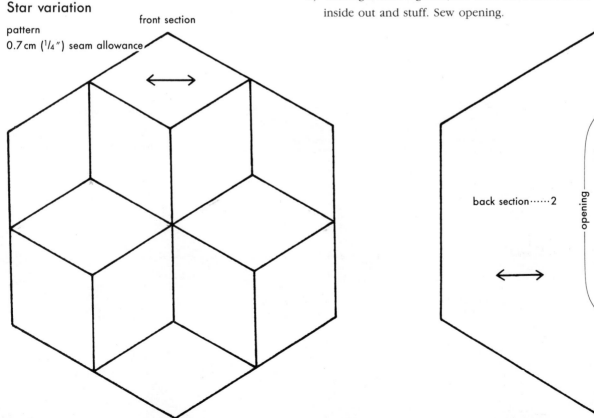

back section······2

opening

Dress covers

Instructions on P. 19

Square variation (actual size)

Materials······Scraps for patchwork, opening section, tab (refer to photo), Lining fabric 90 cm × 20 cm (35½″ × 7⅞″), Thin batting 50 cm × 20 cm (19⅝″ × 7⅞″), 18 cm (7⅛″) zipper
Finished size······Refer to illustration.

Directions

1) Cut fabric. Sew pieces together to make front and back panel.

2) Layer front panel, batting and lining fabric and quilt.

3) Attach opening section and zipper.

4) With right sides together, sew side and bottom seams of front and back panel, inserting tab. Bind seam allowance with lining fabric.

5) Make gusset.

Patterns on P. 37

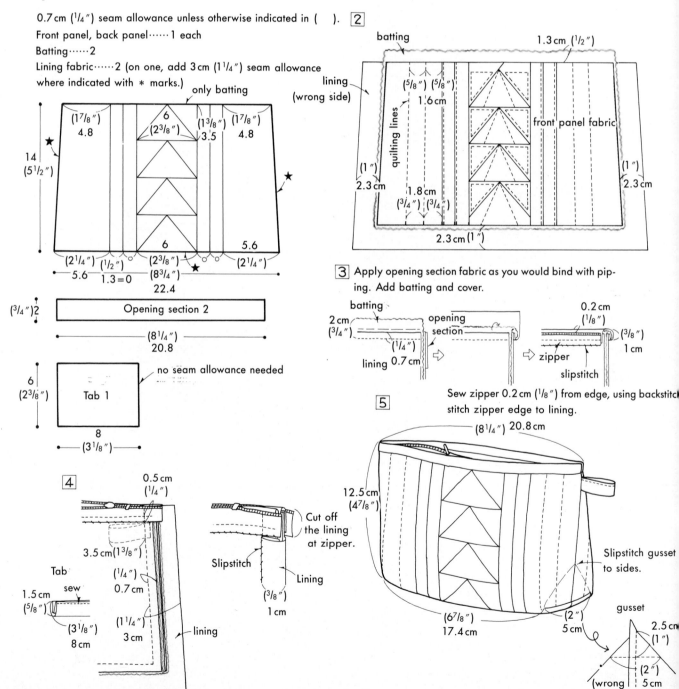

0.7 cm (¼″) seam allowance unless otherwise indicated in ( ).
Front panel, back panel······1 each
Batting······2
Lining fabric······2 (on one, add 3 cm (1¼″) seam allowance where indicated with ✳ marks.)

③ Apply opening section fabric as you would bind with piping. Add batting and cover.

Sew zipper 0.2 cm (⅛″) from edge, using backstitch stitch zipper edge to lining.

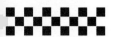
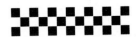
0.7 cm (¹/₄″) seam allowance unless otherwise indicated.

Lid, back section, front section
Cut 1.

no seam allowance needed

3.5
(1³/₈″)

8 (3¹/₈″)

Piping for top edge 1

60
(23⁵/₈″)

bottom

(1³/₈″) 3.5

Piping 1

6
(2³/₈″)

Cut lining fabric and batting 43 cm × 7.5 cm (17″ × 3″)

Materials······Scraps for patchwork and piping (refer to photo), Lining fabric 50 cm × 10 cm (19⁵/₈″ × 4″), Thin batting 50 cm × 10 cm, 1 snap

Finished size······8 cm × 17.5 cm (3¹/₈″ × 6⁷/₈″)

Directions

1) Cut fabric. Sew pieces together.
2) Layer front section, batting and lining. Quilt. Cut corners of lid into a curve.
3) Trim seam allowance on top edge and bind with piping. With wrong sides together, fold and bind edge with piping. Sew on snap.

Patterns on P. 37

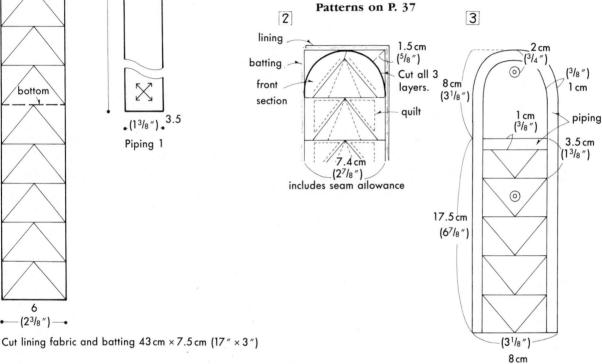

2

lining
batting
front
section

1.5 cm
(⁵/₈″)

Cut all 3 layers.

quilt

7.4 cm
(2⁷/₈″)
includes seam allowance

3

2 cm
(³/₄″)

(³/₈″)
1 cm

8 cm
(3¹/₈″)

1 cm
(³/₈″)

piping

3.5 cm
(1³/₈″)

17.5 cm
(6⁷/₈″)

(3¹/₈″)
8 cm

Sewing Basket and Pincushion

Instructions on P. 66

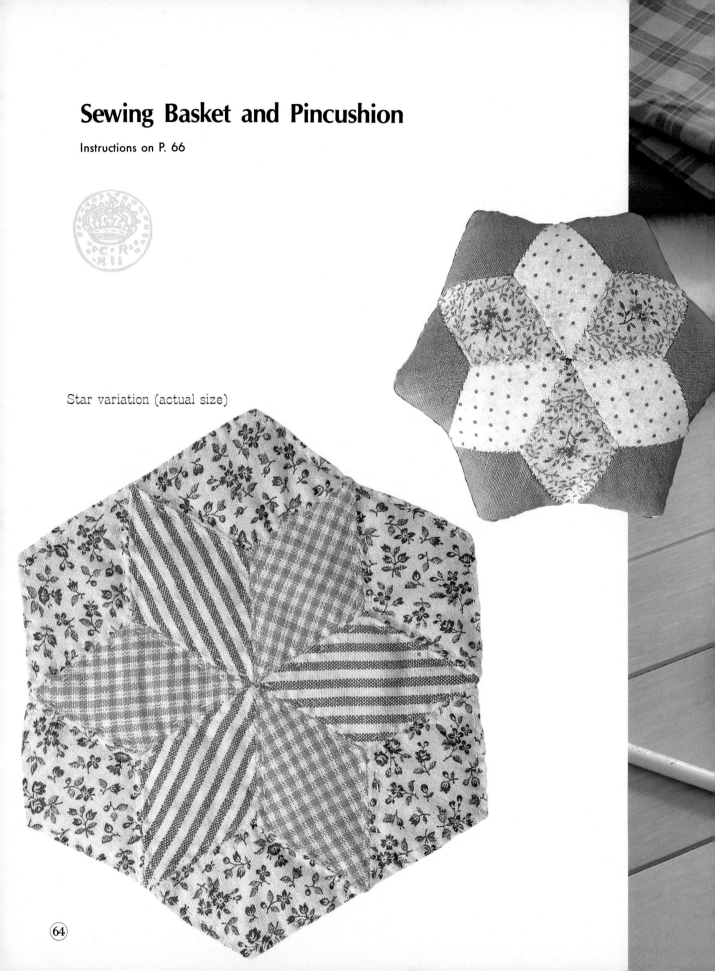

Star variation (actual size)

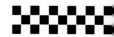
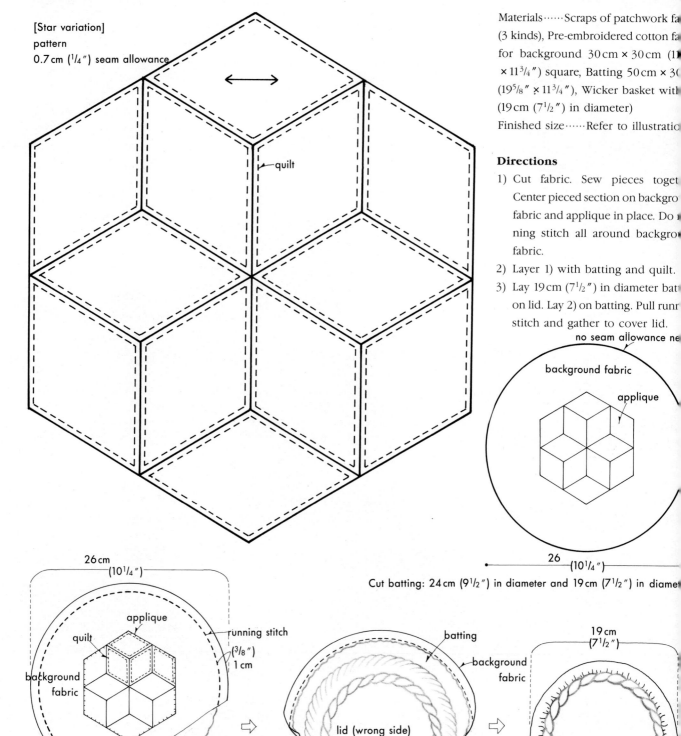

[Star variation]
pattern
0.7 cm ($^1/_4$″) seam allowance

quilt

Materials······Scraps of patchwork fa
(3 kinds), Pre-embroidered cotton fa
for background 30 cm × 30 cm (1
× 11$^3/_4$″) square, Batting 50 cm × 3(
(19$^5/_8$″ × 11$^3/_4$″), Wicker basket with
(19 cm (7$^1/_2$″) in diameter)
Finished size······Refer to illustratio

Directions

1) Cut fabric. Sew pieces toget
   Center pieced section on backgro
   fabric and applique in place. Do
   ning stitch all around backgro
   fabric.

2) Layer 1) with batting and quilt.

3) Lay 19 cm (7$^1/_2$″) in diameter bat
   on lid. Lay 2) on batting. Pull runr
   stitch and gather to cover lid.

no seam allowance ne

background fabric

applique

26
(10$^1/_4$″)

Cut batting: 24 cm (9$^1/_2$″) in diameter and 19 cm (7$^1/_2$″) in diame

26 cm
(10$^1/_4$″)

applique

quilt

running stitch

($^3/_8$″)
1 cm

background
fabric

large

small

batting

lid

(7$^1/_2$″)
19 cm

batting

background
fabric

lid (wrong side)

Fold edges to back.

Gather thread.

19 cm
(7$^1/_2$″)

Cover lid.

Instructions for pincushion is on P. 59

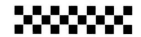

...erials······Scraps of patchwork fabric (4 kinds), Pink print ...ric 90 cm × 40 cm (35$\frac{1}{2}$″ × 15$\frac{3}{4}$″), Red print fabric ...cm × 40 cm (15$\frac{3}{4}$″ × 15$\frac{3}{4}$″) square, Lining fabric ...cm × 20 cm (35$\frac{1}{2}$″ × 7$\frac{7}{8}$″), Thin batting 90 cm × 20 cm, ...stic tape (0.8 cm ($\frac{1}{4}$″) wide) 15 cm (5$\frac{7}{8}$″) ...ished size······Refer to illustration.

...rections
...Cut fabric. Sew pieces together to make side panel. ...Layer side panel, batting and lining fabric. Quilt. Trim ex- ...cess batting and lining fabric. ...cm ($\frac{1}{4}$″) seam allowance unless otherwise indicated in ( ).

3) With right sides together, sew side seam of side panel. Bind seam allowance with lining fabric. Bind bottom edge with pink print fabric.

4) Layer top section, batting and lining. Quilt. Bind opening. For top section, make 2 half circles and position the two to make a circle. Whipstitch 2 cm ($\frac{3}{4}$″) on both ends.

5) With wrong sides together, sew top section and side panel. Bind with red print fabric. Fold 1 cm ($\frac{3}{8}$″) of elastic and attach to bottom.

Patterns on P. 40

Number of pieces required:

a	pink print	16
b	pink print	16
c	red, green, white, pink	4 each

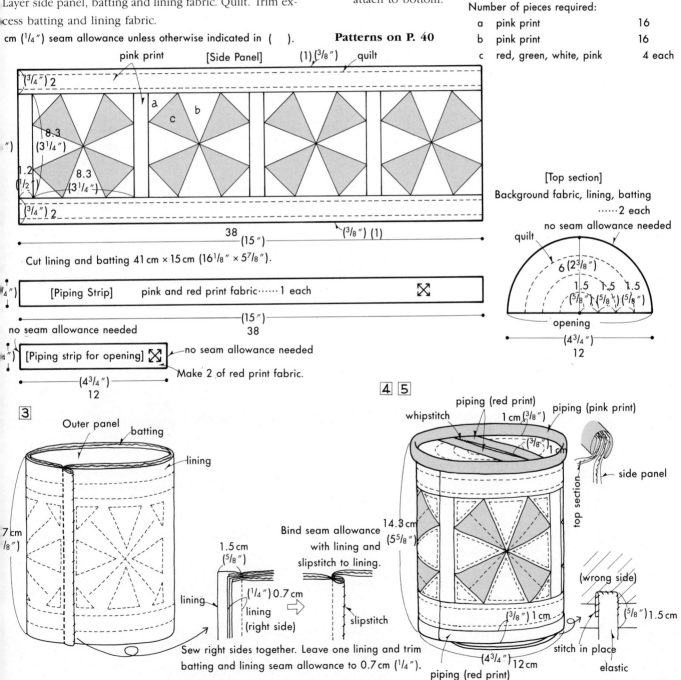

Variety of Tissue Covers:
Roll Paper Cover, Tissue Box Cover, Pocket Tissue Cover

Instructions on PP. 67, 71

Kaleidoscope (actual size)

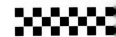
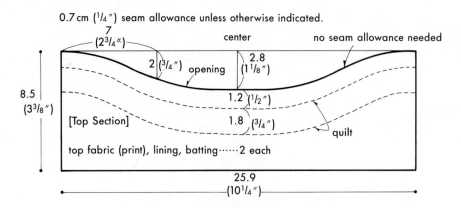

0.7 cm (¹/₄″) seam allowance unless otherwise indicated.

7
(2³/₄″)

center

no seam allowance needed

2 (³/₄″) opening

2.8
(1¹/₈″)

8.5
(3³/₈″)

1.2 (¹/₂″)

1.8 (³/₄″)

[Top Section]

quilt

top fabric (print), lining, batting······2 each

25.9
(10¹/₄″)

1.6
(⁵/₈″)

[Piping strip for opening]   Reddish-brown 2

(10⁵/₈″)
27

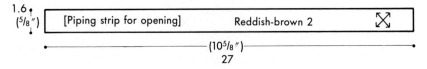

Number of pieces required:
a light olive-green   32
b light olive-green   32
c plaid, green, reddish brown, border   8 each

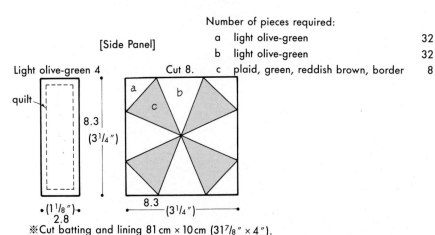

[Side Panel]

Light olive-green 4

quilt

Cut 8.

a

c   b

8.3
(3¹/₄″)

8.3
(3¹/₄″)

(1¹/₈″)
2.8

※Cut batting and lining 81 cm × 10 cm (31⁷/₈″ × 4″).

Materials······Scraps of patchwork fab
kinds), Light olive-green cotton
90 cm × 20 cm (35¹/₂″ × 7⁷/₈″), Print
for top section 60 cm × 10 cm (23⁵/₈″ ×
Reddish-brown cotton fabric 50 cm ×
(19⁵/₈″ × 11³/₄″), Lining fabric 90
20cm, Elastic tape (0.8 cm (¹/₄″)
14 cm (5¹/₂″)

Finished size······Refer to illustration.

Directions

1) Cut fabric. Sew pieces together to
   side panel as shown in illustration

2) Layer 1), batting and lining fabric. (

3) With right sides together, sew side
   of 2). Bind seam allowance with l
   fabric. Bind lower edge with piping
   serting elastic.

4) Layer print fabric for top section, ba
   and lining. Quilt. Bind opening. Fo
   section, make 2 and position as sh
   in illustration. Sew few stitches on
   of opening.

5) Make notches in seam allowance at
   ers of side panel. With right
   together, sew top section and side p
   Trim seam allowance and zigzag ma
   stitch along edge to prevent frayir

Patterns on P. 40

[Placement for Side Panel and Color Order of Piece c]

0.5 cm 2.3 cm   2.3 cm 0.5 cm
(¹/₄″) (1″)   (1″) (¹/₄″)

green reddish-brown border   plaid   green reddish-brown border   plaid

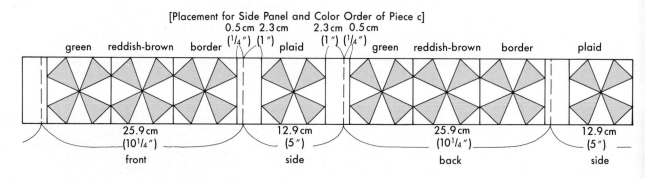

25.9 cm
(10¹/₄″)
front

12.9 cm
(5″)
side

25.9 cm
(10¹/₄″)
back

12.9 cm
(5″)
side

1.6
(⁵/₈″)

[Piping for Bottom Edge]

Reddish-brown 1

78
(30³/₄″) piece if necessary

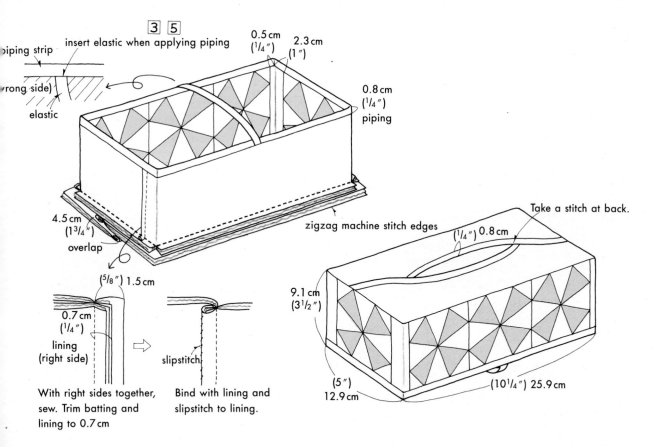

③⑤

insert elastic when applying piping

piping strip

(wrong side)

elastic

0.5 cm (¹/₄″) 2.3 cm (1″)

0.8 cm (¹/₄″) piping

4.5 cm (1³/₄″) overlap

zigzag machine stitch edges

Take a stitch at back.

(¹/₄″) 0.8 cm

9.1 cm (3¹/₂″)

(5″) 12.9 cm

(10¹/₄″) 25.9 cm

(⁵/₈″) 1.5 cm

0.7 cm (¹/₄″)

lining (right side)

With right sides together, sew. Trim batting and lining to 0.7 cm

slipstitch

Bind with lining and slipstitch to lining.

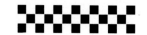

Pocket Tissue Cover······P. 69

Materials (for 1)······Scraps of fabric for patchwork and piping, Lining fabric 20 cm × 20 cm (7⁷/₈″ × 7⁷/₈″), Thin batting ⸱⸱cm × 20 cm

⸱⸱ished size······Refer to illustration.

⸱rections

⸱ Cut fabric. Sew pieces together to make front section.

0.7 cm (¹/₄″) seam allowance unless otherwise indicated ( ).

2) Layer 1), batting and lining fabric. Quilt. Trim excess batting and lining.

3) Bind both ends. Fold right sides together. Take few stitches on both ends. Sew top and bottom. Zigzag machine stitch seam allowances.

Patterns on P. 40

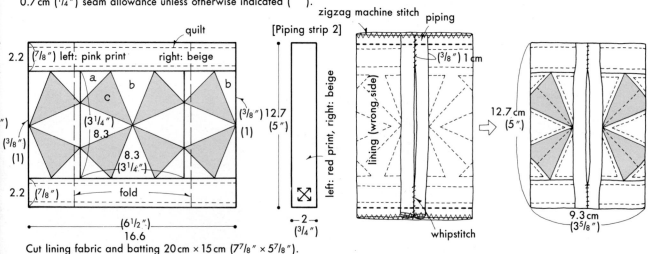

quilt

2.2 (⁷/₈″) left: pink print   right: beige

a b b

c

(3¹/₄″) 8.3

8.3 (3¹/₄″)

(³/₈″) (1)

(³/₈″)12.7 (5″) (1)

2.2 (⁷/₈″) fold

(6¹/₂″) 16.6

Cut lining fabric and batting 20 cm × 15 cm (7⁷/₈″ × 5⁷/₈″).

[Piping strip 2]

left: red print, right: beige

← 2 → (³/₄″)

zigzag machine stitch   piping

lining (wrong side)

(³/₈″) 1 cm

whipstitch

12.7 cm (5″)

9.3 cm (3⁵/₈″)

71

Pouch and Pencil Cases

Instructions on PP. 62, 63

Flying Geese (actual size)